Spotlight on South Korea

Bobbie Kalman

Crabtree Publishing Company

www.crabtreebooks.com

Created by Bobbie Kalman

For my friend Sandra Clubb
You have added good food, good health,
generosity of spirit, and a lot of fun to my life

**Author and
Editor-in-Chief**
Bobbie Kalman

Editors
Kathy Middleton
Crystal Sikkens
Kelly McNiven

Research
Marcella Haanstra

Photo research
Bobbie Kalman

Design
Bobbie Kalman
Katherine Berti
Samantha Crabtree (cover)

Print and production coordinator
Katherine Berti

Photographs
Shutterstock: back cover, pages 1, 3, 4 (t), 5, 6 (map), 7 (t),
   8 (b), 9 (tl, bottom inset), 10, 11 (t), 12, 14 (t), 15 (tl, r),
   16 (t, m), 18 (t), 19 (t), 20 (r), 21, 22, 23, 24 (t), 25 (t),
   26 (tr, br), 27, 28 (t), 29 (tl, tr), 30, 31 (all except tl);
   JinYoung Lee: pages 8–9 (background);
   CHEN WS: cover, pages 11 (b), 20 (l);
   Maxim Tupikov: pages 13 (t), 13 (br); Vacclav: page 13 (bl);
   pcruciatti: page 15 (bl); Gina Smith: pages 25 (b), 28 (b),
   30, 31 (tl); Selfiy: page 29 (br)
Thinkstock: pages 6 (b), 9 (br), 14 (b), 16 (b), 18 (b), 19 (b)
Wikimedia Commons: Doo ho Kim: page 7 (b); William
   Warby: page 17 (l); John Gerrard Keulemans: page 17 (tr);
   Николай Усик: page 17 (br); Jamsong: page 24 (b);
   Kyoushoku: page 26 (l); hojusaram: page 29 (bl)

t=top, b=bottom, m=middle, r=right, l=left, tl=top left,
tr=top right, bl=bottom left, br=bottom right

Library and Archives Canada Cataloguing in Publication

Kalman, Bobbie
      Spotlight on South Korea / Bobbie Kalman.

(Spotlight on my country)
Includes index.
Issued also in electronic format.
ISBN 978-0-7787-0864-3 (bound).--ISBN 978-0-7787-0868-1 (pbk.)

      1. Korea (South)--Juvenile literature. I. Title. II. Series: Spotlight
on my country

DS902.K35 2013   j951.95   C2013-900665-6

Library of Congress Cataloging-in-Publication Data

Kalman, Bobbie.
   Spotlight on South Korea / Bobbie Kalman.
      pages cm. -- (Spotlight on my country)
   Includes index.
   ISBN 978-0-7787-0864-3 (reinforced library binding) -- ISBN 978-0-7787-
0868-1 (pbk.) -- ISBN 978-1-4271-9295-0 (electronic pdf) -- ISBN 978-1-4271-
9219-6 (electronic html)
   1. Korea (South)--Juvenile literature. I. Title.

   DS907.4.K35 2013
   951.95--dc23
                                          2013003287

Crabtree Publishing Company

www.crabtreebooks.com   1-800-387-7650

Printed in the U.S.A./042013/SX20130306

Published in Canada
Crabtree Publishing
616 Welland Ave.
St. Catharines, Ontario
L2M 5V6

Published in the United States
Crabtree Publishing
PMB 59051
350 Fifth Avenue, 59th Floor
New York, New York 10118

Published in the United Kingdom
Crabtree Publishing
Maritime House
Basin Road North, Hove
BN41 1WR

Published in Australia
Crabtree Publishing
3 Charles Street
Coburg North
VIC, 3058

Contents

Where is South Korea?

South Korea is a **country** in east Asia. A country is an area of land with borders. Asia is a large area of land called a **continent**. It is the largest continent in the world. The other continents are Africa, North America, South America, Europe, Australia/Oceania, and Antarctica. The seven continents are on the map below. What are the names of Earth's five oceans?

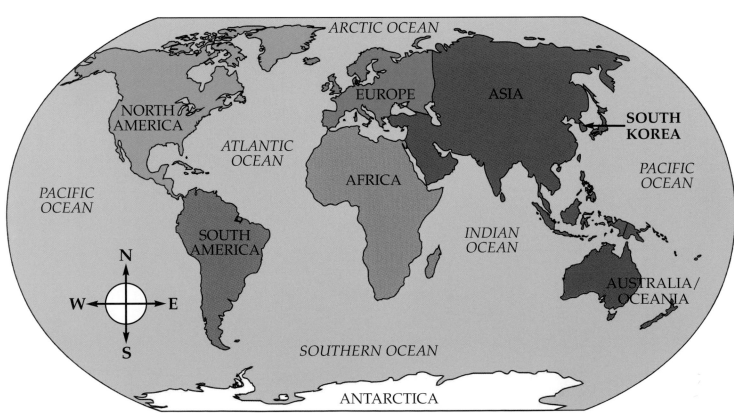

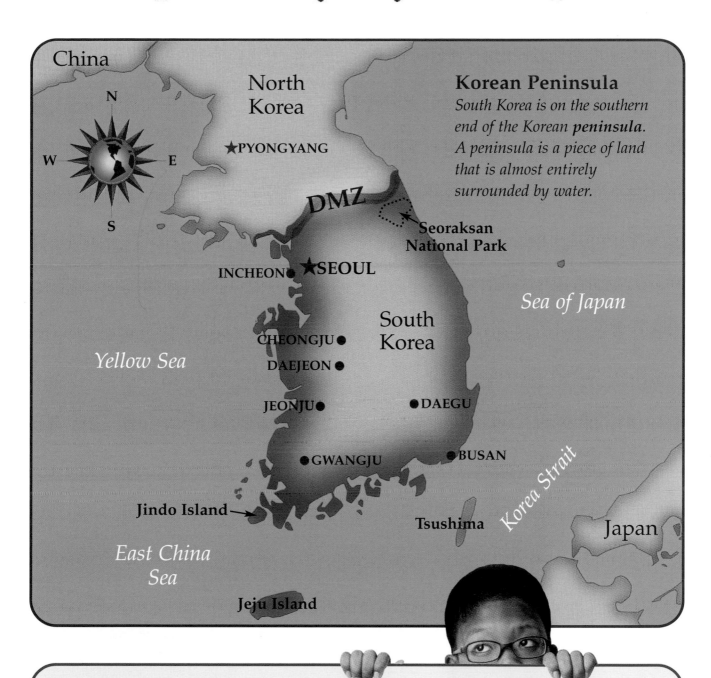

China

North Korea

★PYONGYANG

Korean Peninsula
South Korea is on the southern end of the Korean peninsula. A peninsula is a piece of land that is almost entirely surrounded by water.

N
W · E
S

DMZ

Seoraksan National Park

INCHEON● ★SEOUL

South Korea

Sea of Japan

CHEONGJU●

DAEJEON●

Yellow Sea

JEONJU●

●DAEGU

●GWANGJU

●BUSAN

Korea Strait

Jindo Island →

Tsushima

Japan

East China Sea

Jeju Island

North and South

South Korea's official name is *Hanguk*, or the Republic of Korea. The name "Korea" comes from Goryeo, the name of a **dynasty**, or powerful family, that ruled long ago.

China and Japan are South Korea's neighbors across two seas. South Korea shares a land border with the Democratic People's Republic of Korea, also known as North Korea.

Seas and islands

South Korea is surrounded by three seas: the Sea of Japan, the East China Sea, and the Yellow Sea. Across the Yellow Sea is China. Japan is across the Korea **Strait**, a narrow passage of water that connects two seas. The closest Japanese territory to South Korea is Tsushima Island.

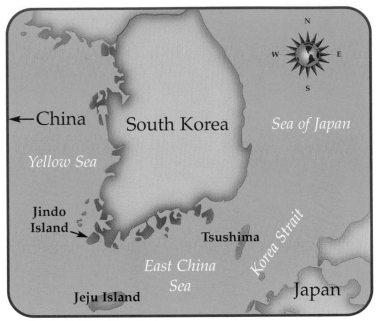

A sea is a part of an ocean that is close to land. The seas near South Korea are part of the Pacific Ocean.

About 3,000 islands belong to South Korea. Most are small and do not have people living on them.

Jeju Island is South Korea's largest island. It is to the south in the East China Sea. Jeju has a warm climate and beautiful landscapes, like this waterfall. It also has a huge **volcano** (see page 9).

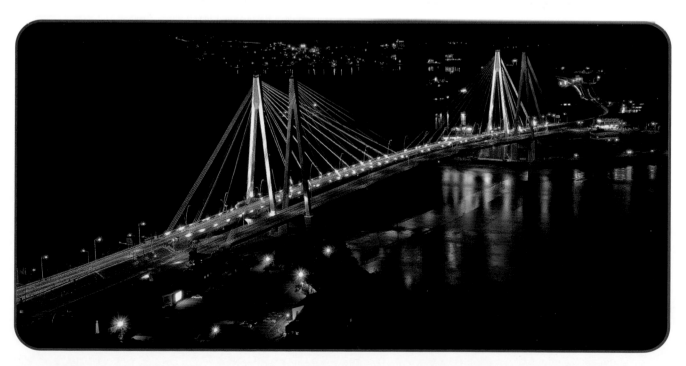

Jindo Island is the third-largest island in South Korea. It is just off the southwest corner of the Korean peninsula. The Myeongnyang Strait is between the island and the mainland. A long suspension bridge now joins the two land areas. The bridge is 1,588 feet (484 meters) long.

Many mountains

Mountains cover almost three-quarters of South Korea. The Taebaek Mountains stretch from the south all the way north into North Korea. Seoraksan is the highest peak in this mountain range at 5,604 feet (1,708 meters) high. The Sobaek Mountains branch off from the Taebaek Mountains. The tallest mountain in the country is Hallasan. It is a volcano located on Jeju Island.

This picture shows a Buddhist temple located in Seoraksan National Park. Behind it is Seoraksan Mountain.

This map shows South Korea's mountains.

Hallasan, on Jeju Island, is South Korea's tallest mountain. It is a **dormant** volcano. The picture above shows Hallasan's **crater**, or pit, at its top.

A long history

Korea is one of the oldest countries in the world. The first Koreans are believed to have **migrated**, or moved, to the Korean Peninsula from northern Asia in 108 BCE. They were farmers who lived in villages and belonged to a large collection of **tribes**, or groups, which came under the control of the Chinese Han Empire. After becoming independent from China, three main kingdoms developed on the Korean Peninsula. They were known as Silla, Baekje, and Goguryo.

Changing rulers

In the 5th, 6th, and 7th centuries, Silla became the most powerful kingdom. In 918, however, all three kingdoms came under the control of a new dynasty called Goryeo. During this period, the religion of Buddhism spread throughout the peninsula (see page 27).

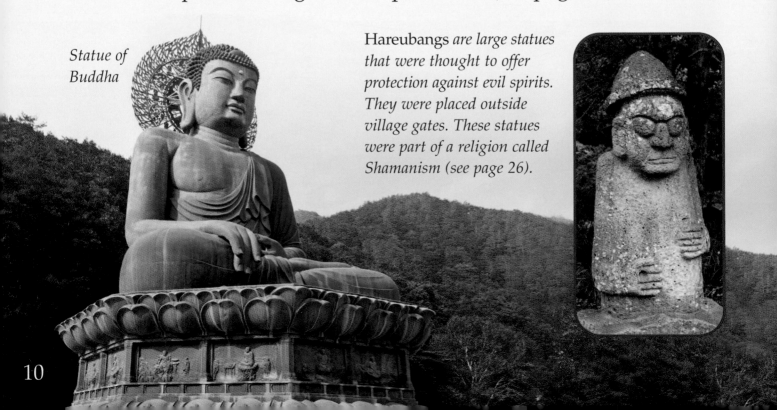

Statue of Buddha

Hareubangs are large statues that were thought to offer protection against evil spirits. They were placed outside village gates. These statues were part of a religion called Shamanism (see page 26).

The Joseon Dynasty

In 1392, the Joseon Dynasty came to power in Korea. Its rulers built a new capital, Hanyang, now Seoul, the capital city of South Korea. Korea remained under the Joseon Dynasty until Japan took it over in 1910.

Sejong the Great was the fourth king of Joseon. He ruled from 1418–1450. He oversaw the creation of hangul, *the native alphabet of the Korean language. He encouraged studies in science and worked hard to make Korea into a wealthy country.*

The Japanese in Korea

The Japanese took away many rights from Koreans. They taught the Japanese language in Korean schools and did not allow Koreans to practice their own **culture**. In 1945, after Japan was defeated in World War II, Korea was finally free of Japanese rule.

Two Koreas

After the war, control of Korea was divided between the United States, who **occupied**, or controlled, the southern part of Korea, and the Soviet Union, who occupied the north. It was at this time that Korea was split into North Korea and South Korea.

The royal guards of the Joseon Dynasty guarded the Gwanghwamun Gate, the entrance to the palace where the king ruled the country (see page 21).

North Korea

The Korean War broke out in 1950 when North Korea invaded South Korea to gain control of the entire peninsula. The war ended in 1953, but a peace treaty was never signed. Today, an unfriendly relationship exists between the two governments. A **demilitarized zone** (DMZ) separates North and South Korea. This strip of land serves as a **buffer zone**, or neutral area, between the two countries. People do not live there, and it has developed into a nature **preserve**.

Total control

In 1948, North Korea's official name became the Democratic People's Republic of Korea, or DPRK. Its capital is Pyongyang, shown in this picture. The government of North Korea is a **totalitarian dictatorship**. A totalitarian government controls every part of a person's life. A dictatorship is run by a ruler who has power over the people of a country. North Korea's ruler is Kim Jong-un.

Children between the ages of 9 and 11 must participate in the Young Pioneers, an organization operated by a **communist** political party. North Korea, however, uses the word Juche instead of "communist" to describe its politics. When they join, the children receive a red tie and pin at a huge celebration.

South Korean soldiers patrol the border in the DMZ between South and North Korea. The two countries are still officially at war.

North Korea has one of the world's largest armies, in which most people must serve.

South Korea today

The national flag of South Korea is called Taegeukgi. *It is white, which represents peace. In the center of the flag is a blue and red symbol of yin-yang, an important part of a religion called Taoism (see page 26). In each corner of the flag is a symbol from a Chinese book called The Book of Changes.*

South Korea is a **republic**. A republic is not ruled by a king or queen but by a leader who is elected by the people. South Korea's president is elected for five years and can serve only one term. In 2013, the first female President, Park Geun-hye, took office. She is assisted in her duties by a prime minister who is appointed by the president.

The Blue House is the office and residence of the South Korean president. It is located in Seoul, the capital city. The Blue House consists of a number of buildings, built in the traditional Korean style.

The won *is the official* **currency**, *or money, of South Korea.*

The official languages of South Korea are Korean and English. Korean is made up of 10 vowels and 14 consonants and is written using symbols. This form of writing is known as Hangul.

South Korea has cold, dry winters and hot, humid summers. August is the most humid month. In most areas of South Korea, the temperature drops below freezing during the winter months. Along the southern coast, it is a bit warmer in the winter.

Korean wildlife

Once there were many bears, lynxes, tigers, and leopards in South Korea, but most have disappeared. Now, many deer populate the land instead. In Seoraksan National Park and the DMZ, however, there are more than 1,500 kinds of wild animals. They include Asian black bears, gorals, musk deer, and otters, shown above right. Tristram's woodpecker, a rare bird, has also been spotted.

South Korea has more than 40 national and provincial parks. Seoraksan National Park has beautiful waterfalls, high mountains, and many kinds of animals that do not live anywhere else in the country. This pair of big pine trees is a symbol of Seoraksan Park.

The Asian black bear is a medium-sized bear that lives in the forests of Seoraksan Park.

Gorals are a cross between goats and antelopes. They live in the DMZ on the Korean Peninsula.

16

vampire teeth

The Tristram's woodpecker is an endangered **species**, or type, of woodpecker that lived in the DMZ but now lives only in North Korea.

(above) Water deer are small deer that are also known as vampire deer because they have a pair of downward pointing teeth. They live in the DMZ.

(right) The Siberian musk deer has a face like a kangaroo. It also has vampire teeth. Instead of antlers, males grow these teeth to attract females.

vampire teeth

Big cities

Seoul is a big city with tall buildings, but it also has beautiful parks and old historic buildings.

Seoul is the capital of South Korea and the biggest city, with a population of close to ten million. Seoul is located in the Southwestern **Plain**, where over half the people in South Korea live. A plain is a large area of flat land. Since the 1960s, more than three-quarters of the people have moved to the cities. Most live in apartment buildings.

The Han River runs through Seoul. Although the city is on a plain, there are mountains around it.

18

Busan is the second-largest city in South Korea. It is located along the southeastern coast. It is the country's major port and fishing center.

Incheon is South Korea's third-largest city. Songdo, shown here, is the business section of Incheon. It has some tall buildings and a busy airport. Incheon is a *free economic zone*, in which companies do not have to pay a lot of taxes.

Famous places

There are some amazing places in South Korea that Koreans love to visit, and people from other countries come to see. Some are national parks with tall mountains, some are historic villages, some are palaces, and others are theme parks. Which places would you like to visit if you were traveling to South Korea?

Dancers in colorful costumes take part in a street parade at Everland, South Korea's largest amusement park. One part, called Magic Land, has restaurants and many kinds of rides, including a log flume, flying ride, and a robot ride. Everland also has a zoo and water park.

Changdeok Palace is located within a large park in Seoul. It is one of the "Five Grand Palaces" built by the kings of the Joseon Dynasty. Changdeok is home to Biwon, or the Secret Garden, which contains over 100 different types of plants, some over 300 years old!

Bukchon Hanok Village in Seoul is home to about 900 traditional houses, called hanok, where people still live. The village has galleries, workshops, and restaurants and is an important center for the arts. It also has a number of museums showing traditional Korean culture.

Gyeongbokgung Palace is the largest of the five palaces in Seoul. It was built by Lee Seong-Gye in 1395, the founding king of the Joseon Dynasty. The main gate, Gwanghwamun, is shown here. Six times a day, the gate guards perform the changing of the guards ceremony and hold a parade. The guards are dressed in colorful costumes and carry traditional weapons and flags.

21

Korean people

This family is wearing traditional clothing called hanbok.

Citizens of South Korea are called Koreans. Almost 49 million people live in South Korea, and almost the entire population belongs to the same **ethnic** group. This means that they share the same appearance and practice the same traditions. A small number of other people also live in South Korea, such as Chinese, Japanese, Americans, and people from Southeast Asia.

Elderly family members are treated with respect.

Koreans have the same kinds of jobs as people in other countries. This woman is a school teacher. She enjoys her job very much.

Most Korean families have one or two children. This family is having fun inline skating together.

Almost every home in South Korea is connected to the Internet, and two-thirds of the people have smart phones or tablets.

The life of children

Children are very important to Koreans, and they place a high value on education. All South Korean children attend the first six grades, and most attend a three-year-long high school. Free education from first grade through high school is provided by the government, but many families hire tutors to help their children get an even better education.

First birthday

When a child turns one in Korea, a big celebration called *dol* is held. The baby is dressed in colorful, fancy clothing called *dol-bok*. At the main celebration, a large table is loaded with different kinds of rice cakes, the main food. Fruit and other foods are also served. The birthday child sits in front of a traditional screen.

Children's Day

Children's Day is a South Korean national holiday celebrated on May 5. Everyone gets involved in the festivities. Many cities have parades and public activities, and museums, zoos, amusement parks, and movie theaters offer free admission to children. Children play traditional games and receive gifts.

Taekwondo demonstrations are often part of Children's Day activities. Taekwondo is a form of self defense that originated in Korea more than 2,000 years ago.

These children are doing a special dance that they learned for Children's Day.

Religions of Korea

The people in South Korea follow different religions, such as Shamanism, Taoism, Buddhism, Confucianism, and Christianity. Buddhist and Confucian beliefs became part of other religions and Korean traditions. Buddha's birthday, for example, is celebrated by the whole country.

Both Taoism and Confucianism were brought to South Korea by the Chinese.

The yin-yang symbol of Taoism shows that everything has two sides that balance each other. This symbol is part of the flag of South Korea.

Christians in South Korea belong to four main religions: Roman Catholic, Presbyterian, Methodist, and Baptist. The church in this picture is a Roman Catholic church.

Shamanism is based on a very old religion. People believe that shamans can heal people or see into the future. These shaman totem poles are meant to scare away evil spirits.

Buddhism

Buddhism began in India about 2,500 years ago. It is based on the teachings of Siddhartha Gautama, a man who became known as the Buddha. Buddhists believe that people should care about all living things and treat them with kindness. Buddhists also believe that they live many lives. Buddhist temples and statues can be found throughout South Korea. This huge Buddha statue and smaller statues are at the Yunwha Mountain Wawoojongsa Temple, located near Seoul. Mountains are a very important part of Korean Shamanism. Korean Buddhism includes many Shamanistic beliefs.

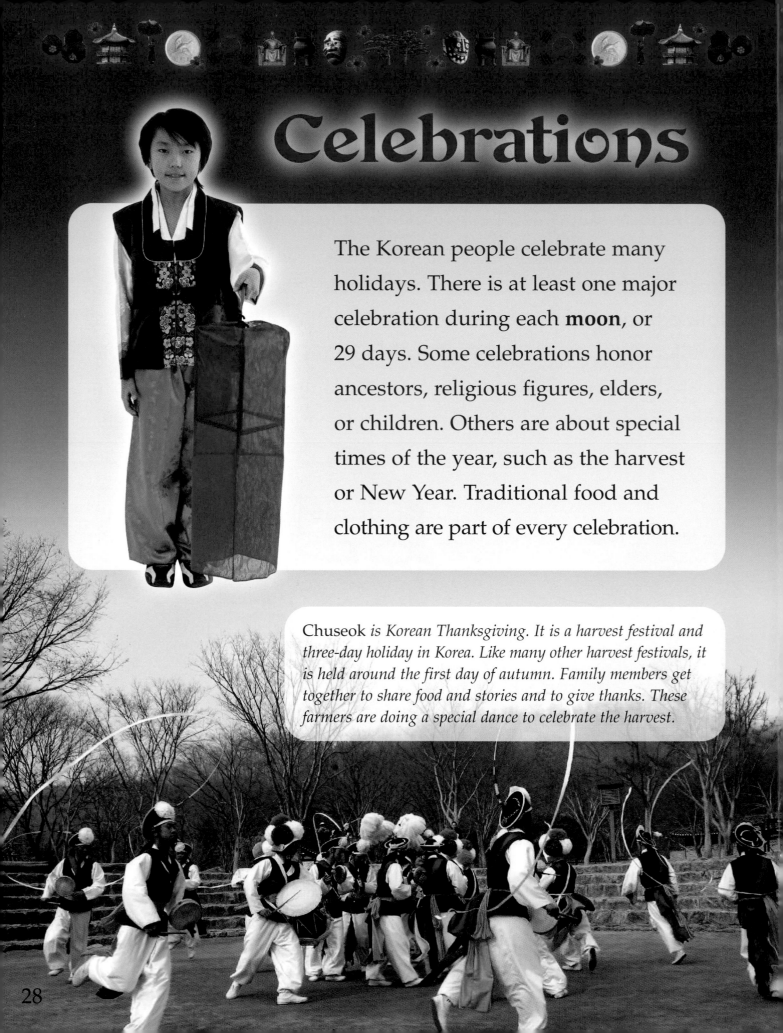

Celebrations

The Korean people celebrate many holidays. There is at least one major celebration during each **moon**, or 29 days. Some celebrations honor ancestors, religious figures, elders, or children. Others are about special times of the year, such as the harvest or New Year. Traditional food and clothing are part of every celebration.

Chuseok is Korean Thanksgiving. It is a harvest festival and three-day holiday in Korea. Like many other harvest festivals, it is held around the first day of autumn. Family members get together to share food and stories and to give thanks. These farmers are doing a special dance to celebrate the harvest.

Korean New Year

The biggest festival in Korea today is *Seollal*, or Korean New Year. It lasts for three days. Family members wish one another good fortune for the coming year. Children receive lucky money, candy, and fruit from their elders. People also fly kites during this festival. They believe that flying a kite takes away bad luck and brings good luck for the new year. Most Koreans wear their traditional clothing during *Seollal*.

Several full-moon festivals are held during the year. The festival shown above, called Daeboreum, *celebrates the first full moon of the year.* Dano *is the spring festival and* Chuseok *is the harvest moon festival.*

The Lotus Lantern Festival is held each May in honor of Buddha's birthday. A spectacular parade shows off huge lanterns in many shapes, including this one, which looks like the Buddha.

29

Korean food

Many Korean meals start with rice, to which a variety of side dishes are added. *Kimchi* is the best-known Korean dish. It is made up of pickled vegetables such as cabbages, cucumbers, radishes, and onions. There are more than 160 different varieties of this dish. Another favorite food is *bibimbap*, a rice dish that includes vegetables, eggs, and a spicy sauce.

Most Korean dishes are made up of rice, meat or fish, vegetables, and sauces.

Kimchi can be made in many ways, but it usually contains cabbage.

People eat their food using chopsticks.

Bibimbap *has an egg in the center.*

Jeon *are pancakes that contain ingredients such as sliced meats, seafood, and vegetables. They are served with a spicy sauce. Some* jeon *pancakes are made with fruit.*

These women sell fresh fish in a market. Many Korean dishes are made with fish and other seafood.

For a fast lunch, people make instant noodle soups and add their own veggies and meat.

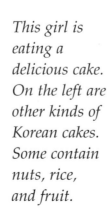

This girl is eating a delicious cake. On the left are other kinds of Korean cakes. Some contain nuts, rice, and fruit.

Glossary

Note: Some boldfaced words are defined where they appear in the book.

buffer zone A neutral area used to separate two hostile countries

communist Describing a political system in which everything is owned and directed by the government

crater A pit or bowl-shaped opening at the top of a volcano

culture The beliefs, customs, and ways of life of a group of people

dormant Describing a volcano that has not erupted in a very long time

dynasty A line of related powerful rulers of a country

ethnic Describing people with a common national or cultural tradition

migrate To move to another place

occupied Having taken control of an area

peninsula A piece of land that has water almost all the way around it

plain A flat area of land with a few trees

preserve A natural area set aside by a country's government to protect the plants and animals living there

species A group of closely related living things that can make babies together

strait A narrow area of water that connects two large areas of water

tribe A group of people who shares ancestors, beliefs, customs, and leaders

volcano An opening in Earth's crust where hot lava, gases, ash, and rocks shoot out; a mountain formed from the lava and rocks

Index